Inside Animal Homes

Inside
Bird Nests

Ethan Danielson

New York

Published in 2016 by The Rosen Publishing Group, Inc.
29 East 21st Street, New York, NY 10010

First Edition

Editor: Sarah Machajewski
Book Design: Mickey Harmon

Photo Credits: Cover, p. 1 (birds) FloridaStock/Shutterstock.com; cover, pp. 3, 4, 6, 8, 10, 12, 14, 16, 18, 20, 22–24 (hay) Chaikovskiy Igor/Shutterstock.com; cover, pp. 1, 3, 4, 6–12, 14, 16, 18–20, 22–24 (magnifying glass shape), musicman/Shutterstock.com; p. 5 Paul Nicklen/National Geographic/Getty Images; p. 7 (water nest) Stacy Ann Alberts/Shutterstock.com; p. 7 (owl) Wayne Lynch/All Canada Photos/Getty Images; p. 7 (woven nest) Dave Montreuil/Shutterstock.com; p. 9 (main) Marc Moritsch/National Geographic/Getty Images; p. 9 (inset) Elliotte Rusty Harold/Shutterstock.com; p. 11 (inset) Twenty20 Inc/Shutterstock.com; p. 11 (main) Emi/Shutterstock.com; p. 13 (penguin) Tshooter/Shutterstock.com; p. 13 (eagle) Phillip Rubino/Shutterstock.com; p. 15 kojihirano/Shutterstock.com; p. 17 (main) EcoPrint/Shutterstock.com; p. 17 (bird) Sam DCruz/Shutterstock.com; p. 19 (main) http://upload.wikimedia.org/wikipedia/commons/8/8b/Natural_Bird%27s_Nest_in_Thai_Bird%27s_Nest_Island..jpg; p. 19 (inset) feathercollector/Shutterstock.com; p. 21 wizdata/Shutterstock.com; p. 22 INSAGO/Shutterstock.com.

Manufactured in the United States of America

CPSIA Compliance Information: Batch #WS15PK: For Further Information contact Rosen Publishing, New York, New York at 1-800-237-9932

Contents

Different Homes 4

Around the World 6

Bird Bodies 8

All About Beaks 10

Bird Wings 12

Building Nests 14

Making a Home 16

Location, Location, Location 18

Babies in the Nest 20

Stay Away! 22

Glossary 23

Index 24

Websites 24

Different Homes

Homes are a big part of people's lives. They're a place to live and stay safe from **conditions** outside. People live in small homes, big homes, homes in cities, and homes in the country. Our homes can be made of wood, brick, glass, and more.

People aren't the only creatures that build homes. Birds build homes, too, though theirs are much different from ours. Let's take a closer look at how birds live.

THE INSIDE SCOOP

What's the biggest home you've seen? The biggest bird nest was built in 1963 by a pair of bald eagles. It was almost 10 feet (3 m) wide and 20 feet (6 m) deep! Scientists think it weighed about 4,409 pounds (2,000 kg).

How is this eagle's home different from yours?

Around the World

Birds live everywhere. There are about 10,000 different species, or kinds, of birds, and they live all over the world. They can be found in our neighborhoods, but they also live in extreme places such as Antarctica and the sides of mountains. Snowy owls north of the Arctic Circle build nests on raised ground, where the wind blows away all the snow.

The kinds of birds that live in one place aren't always found in another. Different bird species have **adaptations** that have allowed them to live in certain **habitats**.

These birds live in different areas of the world. This affects what their nests are like.

Bird Bodies

Birds come in many shapes and sizes, but they share the same features. All birds have two feet, a beak, two wings, and feathers. However, the way these parts look and the way they're used can be very different. They tell us a lot about how birds live.

Small birds such as robins and blue jays have feet made for walking and **perching**. Water birds such as ducks and penguins have feet that are good for swimming. **Birds of prey**, such as owls and eagles, have feet with sharp claws that help them catch their dinner.

THE INSIDE SCOOP

The smallest living bird is the bee hummingbird. It's about 2.5 inches (6.4 cm) long. The largest living bird is the ostrich. Some have been measured to stand 9 feet (2.7 m) tall!

bee hummingbird

Some birds dig nests called burrows in the ground.
They use their feet to push the dirt away
as they're building.

All About Beaks

The shape and size of a bird's beak can also tell a lot about how it lives. Beaks are used for eating. Short, rounded beaks help some birds, such as cardinals, crack nuts and seeds. A hummingbird's long, thin beak helps it sip nectar from flowers. A pelican's big, deep beak is great for scooping up fish!

Birds also use their beak to build their nest. They pick up sticks, straw, and other building **materials** and carry them back to their home.

THE INSIDE SCOOP

Woodpeckers use their beak as a nest-building tool. They knock their beak against wood until they create a hole. Then, they use their beak and tongue to clear the inside of wood and bugs.

woodpecker

A blackbird uses its beak to gather materials for its nest.

Bird Wings

A bird's most familiar feature may be its wings. Most birds use their wings to fly. Wings are made of **muscles** and bones that work together to pull a wing up and down. Muscles give birds strength to fly. The way feathers are shaped and ordered allows birds to keep themselves in the air.

Even though all birds have wings, not all birds can fly. Penguins are flightless birds that use their wings as flippers. Ostriches can't fly, either—they use their wings for balance when running.

Birds are covered in feathers. Feathers keep birds dry and **protect** against heat and cold. Some birds shed their feathers once a year, which is called molting.

13

Building Nests

Nests are an important part of birds' survival because they keep eggs and chicks safe. Birds are good nest builders because they have many body parts to help them build. They use their feet and beak to carry materials. They use their wings to flatten, smooth, or dig nests.

Some birds build nests using materials found in nature. Cavity nesters, such as the European starling, nest in **structures** that already exist, such as holes in buildings! The burrowing owl lives in—you guessed it—burrows. These are just a few examples.

THE INSIDE SCOOP

Auks and murres lay their eggs directly on rocks. They don't build nests out of natural materials like other bird species.

Many birds in deserts, or hot, dry habitats, build their nest inside a cactus! Gila woodpeckers poke a hole in the cactus with their beak, and then they hollow it out.

Making a Home

Birds use the materials available in their habitat to build nests. Materials could include twigs, sand, grass, leaves, and anything else that looks good for nest building. Birds **arrange** these materials into bowl shapes to keep their eggs from rolling out.

Some bird nests are simple. A nest called a scrape is just a dent in the ground. However, some bird nests are very **complex**. Sociable weavers build nests with enough room to house up to 400 birds! These nests have entrances, roofs, and inside walls lined with soft plant materials.

THE INSIDE SCOOP

Female great hornbills build nests, then seal the inside walls with their own poop! Nothing can get in but food, which the male great hornbill delivers through a small hole in the nest.

Sociable weavers work hard to care for their nest. They're always adding new material to keep it in good condition. You can even hear them calling to each other while they work.

Location, Location, Location

When you think of a bird's nest, you may picture a pile of twigs in a tree or on its branches. However, birds can build their nests almost anywhere.

Cliff swallows build nests on the sides of cliffs. American coot nests are often piles of sticks in the middle of water. Bird nests can be found under bridges, in barns, and on the sides of buildings. The only thing that matters is that predators can't reach it. The nest must be high enough or hidden enough from animals that hunt the birds.

nests

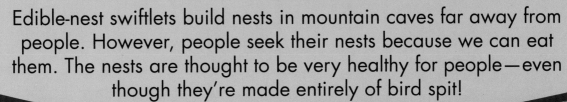

Edible-nest swiftlets build nests in mountain caves far away from people. However, people seek their nests because we can eat them. The nests are thought to be very healthy for people—even though they're made entirely of bird spit!

Babies in the Nest

Once a nest has been built, birds have one job to do: lay eggs! Most birds lay between 3 and 5 eggs during their laying season, but it can be different based on species.

Birds sit on their eggs to keep them warm, which helps the chicks grow. After the chicks break out of their shell, they stay safely in the nest. They can't see or fly at first. Their parents bring food to the nest until the chicks are old enough to leave.

THE INSIDE SCOOP

Kingbirds, blue jays, mockingbirds, and magpies are very protective of their young. If a predator comes close to the nest, they will dive at it or flap their wings until it goes away.

Bird parents find food and bring it back to their young. When they come back to the nest, the chicks raise their neck and open their mouth wide for food!

Stay Away!

If there's one thing to be learned from studying bird nests, it's that the 10,000 species of birds alive today are all very different. The way a nest looks depends on what kind of bird made it as well as where and how the bird lives.

If you see a bird nest in your area, stay away! Birds don't like when people get too close, and they may not return to the nest if you touch it. Staying away from nests helps birds stay safe.

Glossary

adaptation: A change that helps a living thing live best in its habitat.

arrange: To put things in order.

bird of prey: A bird that hunts other animals for food.

complex: Consisting of many different parts.

condition: The state of something.

habitat: The natural home of a plant, animal, or other living thing.

material: The matter from which something is made.

muscle: A body part that produces movement.

perch: To rest on something.

protect: To keep safe.

structure: A building or other object.

Index

A
American coot, 18
auks, 14

B
beak, 8, 10, 11,
    14, 15
blackbird, 11
burrowing owl, 14
burrows, 9, 14

C
cavity nesters, 14
chicks, 14, 20, 21
cliff swallows, 18

E
eagles, 4, 5, 8
edible-nest swiftlets,
    19
eggs, 14, 16, 20
European starling, 14

F
feathers, 8, 12
feet, 8, 9, 14

G
Gila woodpecker, 15
great hornbills, 16

H
habitats, 6, 15, 16

M
materials, 10, 11, 14,
    16, 17
murres, 14

S
scrape, 16
sociable weavers,
    16, 17
species, 6, 14,
    20, 22

W
wings, 8, 12, 14, 20
woodpeckers, 10, 11

Websites

Due to the changing nature of Internet links, PowerKids Press has developed an online list of websites related to the subject of this book. This site is updated regularly. Please use this link to access the list: www.powerkidslinks.com/home/bird